MEDICAL MARKETING

DEMYSTIFIED

LEVERAGE THE INTERNET TO GROW YOUR PRACTICE IN 5 EASY STEPS

TONY MORK, M.D.

MEDICAL MARKETING
DEMYSTIFIED

Medical Marketing Demystified

Copyright © 2014 by Tony Mork, MD

www.MedicalWebsiteAcademy.com

ISBN-13: 978-0-9860770-0-5 (cloth)
ISBN-13: 978-0-9860770-1-2 (paperback)
ISBN-13: 978-0-9860770-2-9 (ebook)

CONTENTS

INTRODUCTION

As a physician, I've been fascinated with the explosion of technology in the past twenty years. Some of this technology has made it easier to diagnose and treat my patients. Online technology, on the other hand, has been a little harder to keep up with. For generations, physicians were trained in science, chemistry, biology, anatomy and healing. With the healthcare system in turmoil and competition for patients heating up, no physician can survive economically in the coming years without continuing to add to his or her knowledge base. Specifically, I am talking about online marketing.

Medical Marketing Demystified is designed to be your wake-up call, your guide and your new reference book for your twenty-first century medical practice. Inside these pages, you'll learn new terms like "autoresponder" and "SEO." By the time you are done digesting this information, you'll know more than 90 percent of your competitors.

A word of caution, however. As the famous saying goes, "To know and not to do is yet not to know." As you begin to understand the ins and outs of a medical website, search engine basics and how to establish a larger online presence, take a moment each week and put into motion the Action Steps at the end of each chapter.

At first glance, this information may seem overwhelming . The deeper we go, the more questions may arise. In my case, my thirst to learn and serve pulled me to medicine. This same desire to discover was equally compelling in my journey as a medical marketing expert. As you go through this book (and then perhaps the companion courses offered on www.MedicalWebsiteAcademy.com), set a pace that your schedule allows. Above all else, don't do it alone.

Like a hospital with dozens of specialists, your online presence cannot be built alone. I'll show you how to hire the right team to design your website, acquire new patients, manage the process and create a royalty-based income that can, quite possibly, set you free financially.

It doesn't matter if your goal is simply to increase production expand your practice or to become the next Dr. Oz, you will begin this initiative with a functional and relevant website. Your website will be the hub of the wheel of your medical presence online.

Once your site is designed, we'll go through the options to set up the "spokes" of your wheel – ensuring that new potential patients find you, educating them once they do and using a blog to share patient stories (testimonials) – all with the goal of getting qualified referrals.

You've invested a fortune to become a physician. More importantly, you've invested your life. If you were to count the hours spent at medical school, your internship and countless sleepless nights on call or studying for your CME credits, you may realize that you've probably invested more of your life than any other profession. Your investment is precious...and it is in jeopardy.

Concierge medicine, hospital conglomerates, the Affordable Care Act, managed care, Medicare and dozens of other moving targets are changing the landscape of your practice faster than you can likely keep up. Physicians who do not embrace the Internet as a serious business tool, or those that put their heads in the sand and ignore building an online presence, will see their livelihoods shrink, or worse...evaporate.

It is the forward-thinking physician who not only survives but thrives when the dynamics change. You may label yourself a healer, doctor or surgeon, but what keeps the lights on and the mortgage paid are your skills as a businessperson.

Unfortunately, most physicians don't have solid online entrepreneurial experience and rely solely on their medical business skills. If we think we don't need to acquire new business skills, we simply won't be well-equipped to make important business decisions.

Your medical skills have provided you status and immediate income. But your new online business skills will keep the cash flow healthy and ever increasing.

Read through this book at a pace you can keep. Take notes. Refer back to it as often as you want but, most importantly, you must take action.

At the risk of sounding dramatic, the life of your practice depends on it.

CHAPTER ONE

YOUR WEBSITE—THE GAME LEVELER

When it comes to websites, your appearance to the world can be the same as or better than the Mayo Clinic.

PURPOSE OF A MEDICAL WEBSITE

The Internet is the greatest leveler of the "game field" of business and commerce that has occurred in our lifetime. Can you imagine the feeling of being able to advertise to millions of people for free and to be able to have the same look and feel as the Mayo Clinic or Apple? It would have been unthinkable just a few years ago for a small business owner to disrupt or challenge the likes of a Fortune 1000 company. Today it is commonplace.

Giants like Facebook, Groupon and thousands of other startups catch fire and grow exponentially, not as the result of a multimillion-dollar ad campaign, but because of the power and speed of online communication.

As a physician, you've witnessed the political and corporate disruption of your practice. While it may be futile to fight city hall, it is imperative that you embrace the cultural trends of communication, business and social behaviors of your patients and use them to your advantage. In other words, you must have a website.

And, your website must improve. To be clear, even if you already have a website, it requires updating on a consistent basis. Most likely it is not functioning optimally, and you may be missing out on hundreds of thousands of dollars in incremental revenue.

The purpose of a medical website is threefold:

1. To provide a place where people can find you

2. To provide value to visitors

3. To collect names and email address of visitors

Fortunately, with the click of a mouse, you have the same opportunity to present yourself to the world as any large company does. Miraculously, with the right structure, content and consistent look and feel, you can impact thousands of potential patients and clients for free. The whole world can now see and get to know you and engage with your practice...online. Within a few weeks, you can advertise your services and even monetize the products of others as effectively as the Mayo Clinic or Jenny Craig.

Unlike traditional advertising, where businesses pay obscene dollars for placements in print, radio or television, the Internet provides a vehicle for clients and patients to search for your services and products. Instead of pushing your brand and offerings to someone, they seek *you* out.

By creating a "pull" as opposed to a "push" marketing machine, you will intelligently place your website, content, education and experience directly in the path of potential patients. Your medical website will be an information portal and marketing platform.

Creating a functional and compelling online presence can become more than a financial lifeboat in a sea of turmoil. Your medical website can become a very healthy and robust residual income stream for you and your family.

TEAM CAPTAIN, COACH, PLAYERS AND THE WATER BOY

You've probably considered or may have already created some sort of website for your practice. Regardless of whether you have a website, take a step back and ask yourself the following questions:

- What is the purpose of your website?

- How does your website fit into your medical practice?

- How do you measure your intent against the results?

This book is designed to provide a framework and strategy to help you create a website that's not only functional but will also work for you 24/7—connecting with existing patients, educating potential patients...and even becoming a cash machine that creates residual income by selling products you don't even manufacture.

In my fourteen years having an Internet-based medical practice, I have always been a physician. During this time, I've had great online marketing successes and a healthy dose of failures. For many of those years, I simply wanted someone else tell me what to do. Like you, I had no time to learn a new career. On top of that, marketing technology changes at a rapid pace. It is impossible to keep up with all of it.

I was spending a lot of money and wasn't sure about the benefit I was getting. I was unsure that the people I'd hired to design and run my site knew about the challenges of a medical practice. My "spider sense" began to tingle as I spent thousands on courses, products and systems that appeared "cool" but, in the end, didn't accomplish anything measurable. After fourteen years and tens of thousands of dollars, I've amassed a considerable amount of practical knowledge, not simply of Internet marketing, but of Internet marketing for our medical industry.

In that time, I arrived at a few conclusions. One conclusion I reached was that no single individual or skill can build an effective website or online presence.

In every single case, a full and diverse team is required to do this properly. Pardon the sports analogy, but for the first few years, I was acting as coach, player, captain and water boy. Doing it all was driving me crazy.

When it comes to building your online business, you will still have more than one role, but you won't be doing it alone.

You are the team owner. The buck stops with you. Be sure to have a clear budget. Moreover, have a conservative, mid-range and "homerun" goal for revenue creation. Projecting new income is fun! But do so with conservative figures. It's been said that, once you have a budget and goals in place, you should double the expenses, halve the revenue and see how it feels then. Many of our patients are clients for years. The lifetime value of a patient and their family can be in the tens of thousands of dollars. Don't simply look at the short-term income of a particular procedure, supplement, or billable code. Every patient has family, friends and many health-related needs.

Who are your team players? The first is a website designer.

There are hundreds of thousands of website templates. For a few hundred bucks, you can copy a template, input your information and have a website.

Yawn.

What about the purpose? What do you want the user experience to be? Website designers and website developers will not always know much about marketing a medical practice. While certain marketing concepts are universal, there are some techniques that definitely don't work when marketing a medical practice online.

As the team owner, it is your job to have a clear goal regarding your practice and how your website will support or even lead those goals.

- Do you want to offer non-insurance services?

- Are you interested in getting more referrals?

- Would you like to expand or open up your own clinic?

Sit back and write down specific six-month, and one- and five-year goals for your practice. What do you really want to achieve? Don't limit yourself to your present reality. Your website can open up doors you didn't even know existed. Get clear on your goals, and you'll be able to better communicate them to your team.

Internet marketing experts may excel at general online marketing but be unable to apply their knowledge effectively to a medical practice. The language or "speak" of Internet experts can also be difficult to understand. I've kept this book simple on purpose, but you may find words and phrases that are new to you. Refer to the

Glossary at the back if you need help.

Your team should design and execute an integrative strategy that blends online, offline and social media efforts.

A good website will help generate trust with potential patients and will facilitate scheduling an appointment.

A great website will educate them to such a degree that they won't bother looking anywhere else.

In either case, your website is the result of a team effort from experts that specialize in web design and development, search engine optimization (SEO for short) and video. You own the team and will act as captain (and occasionally, water boy), but you will choose individual players with a wide variety of skills: technical, design, interpersonal communication, traditional marketing, customer service and sales.

The creation and execution of a functional website is so far out of the physician's normal experience and training that you may not know what you really need, and there is a lot of opportunity to overpay.

Before you invest another dollar in your website, online strategy or new marketing initiative, it is critical to learn the playbook of medical marketing online. Before you hire your players, let's look at the functional intent of your website.

FOR WHOM IS YOUR WEBSITE?

It's easy to create a site about the owner and his or her credentials or to show a picture of the office building and waiting area. That's easy but not compelling. This type of site is referred to as a "brochure" or "vanity" site.

People who visit your site are interested in only one thing: themselves. Although your credentials are important, they are not the primary concern of someone visiting your site. Visitors are looking to see if you can solve their problems.

No one searches for credentials. They always start by seeking information about and solutions to their problem. Once they feel you have answered their questions and have the background and experience to help them, they may then verify your credentials. But, your problem-solving skills and the social proof of your success are vastly more important than your degrees.

This single concept of designing, writing and positioning your site for the user is the driving force behind your medical website and your entire online presence.

From now and forever, think about the following phrase when creating a video, writing a blog post or evaluating your copy:

"How can I help you solve your problem?"

If you master this single concept, you'll be head and shoulders above the competition.

DESIGN YOUR WEBSITE FOR "THE SEARCH"

When you sit back and consider the intent of your medical website, think about how to make it easy for potential patients to:

1. Find answers to their problems.

2. Contact you

In other words, is your contact information clearly on display? Think about your own frustrations when you search a website and can't easily find what you're looking for.

eBay became a giant in online shopping because it created an online garage sale with billions in valuation. From shoes to airplanes, there is nothing that can't be bought or sold on eBay.

Try to get eBay's customer service department on the phone. Dead end. They don't have one. All of their "service" is done via email.

This model works for the grandest garage sale on the Internet, but it is unlikely to work for a thriving medical practice.

At the opposite end of the spectrum is online shopping giant

Zappos. Zappos plasters their 800 number on every single web-page. They don't simply have robust customer service. Their value proposition *is* their service. They want you to call them. Zappos realized early on that their sales increased and customer retention soared the more their customers engaged with them on the phone. That's old school brilliant.

When it comes to your medical site, make it brain-dead simple for potential patients and clients to contact you. You don't need a call center staffed 24/7, but your practice needs to be accessible.

A potential patient looking at your website is trying to solve a problem, so make it easy for them. You've seen confusing websites. You look, search and are quickly lost in a sea of content, ads or fluff.

But your site won't do that. You'll understand the interest and intent of your potential patients, and, with a properly-designed site, you'll make it easy for them to engage.

The simpler the better.

This seems like a straight-forward proposition, but there are two sides to it, and one of them is invisible. It's easy enough to imag-ine how your website looks, because it is visible to you (the "fron-tend"). While it is important that your website's frontend is attractive and makes it easy for patients to find what they're looking for, that's not all. The way your website is constructed (the "backend") is not visible but is also very important. This architecture will influence how eas-ily people will be able to find the information that you provide on your website when they're searching for something on Google or another search engine.

Searching the Internet is much more arcane than looking through the Yellow pages of the phone book and can change dramatically when search engines change their algorithms. You need to know about these algorithm changes and respond to them in a timely manner. But who tells you these things?

Think of how your potential patient might start his or her In-ternet search, in order to find out more about his or her problem. What are your potential patients going to type into Google? What problems are they trying to solve?

This is important because you may or may not want to create a website (or websites) based on your personal name or geographic location. The closer your URL (www.____.com) resembles what your patient is searching for, the more relevant it becomes to the search engines. The URL is the name you choose when you pick a name for your website. The URL has the highest priority with respect to the searched term, so the closer your URL matches what your patients will be searching for, the easier it will be for them to find you. The closer your URL is to the words or phrase of the service you offer, the more likely the search engines will find you. If you're in Chicago and specialize in throat cancer, www. throat-cancerspecialtychicago.com may be a good domain. If you have patients coming from beyond your city limits, you would drop the city from your URL.

TERMS, LAYOUT AND COLORS

Once you have purchased a URL, someone will have to host it, in order for it to "go live" on the Internet. There are a variety of options for hosting, such as GoDaddy, MediaTemple and Hostgator. Or, your web designer may be able host it for you. We list our top hosting choices in the Resources section at the end of this book.

The header is the next section of your website that deserves attention, After your URL, it is the next part of your website that the search engines will look to when crawling your site for search terms (also known as keywords). The header is at the top of your website. Some keywords will be visible to you (on the frontend); some will only be visible to the search engines (on the backend).

This is where quality web construction can maximize the possibility of a potential patient finding your site when they search the Internet.

There is a particular organization pattern that will increase the appeal and functionality of your medical website to a potential patient searching for your services. The organization and placement of information should be based on how the eye moves when it looks at a webpage. In Western cultures, the eye generally moves from top-left, down and then to the right. Understanding how the eye moves should dictate the placement of important information on the pages of your website. You have a very short amount of time to get someone's attention and keep it. An experienced web designer can help people stay on your site. (If you are interested in creating your own website, you can use the free platform that WordPress (WP) offers.)

Think of a website like a folded newspaper. When you pick up a newspaper and look at it, you will see the top half of the front page. When you unfold the paper, you will see the bottom half. It is the same when you open and look at a website. What you see first is considered "above the fold," and you must scroll down to see what is "below the fold." Your most engaging information must be placed above the fold. To keep your visitor engaged, you must provide some value right away. A potential patient doesn't care about what your medical office looks like; he or she is looking for the answer to a problem.

Your website copy must immediately describe the problem the potential patient has (in plain English) and start to offer a solution. The patient will never get below the fold if they don't like or relate to what's above it.

Everyone likes a website that is simple, clean and easy to navigate. It should have a consistent "look and feel" to it. Websites that are too busy, dark or confusing to look at are instant turn-offs.

Your website should be designed with your patient population in mind. If your population is older, provide a large phone number that is easy to see and don't ask them to book appointments online when they can barely send an email. If you are an OB/GYN, your color selection, fonts and copy should lean to the feminine side.

Some websites are a little more structured and business-like, while others are a bit more free-form. No matter what your choice is, the same basic components are needed.

Above the fold, ensure that you have these three components on your website:

Header, tagline and contact information. This content should be created and displayed in text format, not graphically. Search engines can read text but not the text in a graphic. If you use a graphic, be sure your designer embeds the proper tags to the image. Tags help boost your ranking in the search engines.

Informational video. Today's Internet is quickly becoming the family television. People are quite comfortable with video online and even expect it. Make your "welcome video" short, punchy and authentic. You don't need to take acting lessons, but you should be relatable, enthusiastic and concise. If you are nervous, simply talk to the camera as if you were sharing something with a good friend. Or, just narrate a PowerPoint presentation.

Opt-in form. You've seen these before: "Enter your name and email for a free report." Your opt-in form is your first shot at engaging and educating your potential patient, without using up your valuable time. Later, we'll discuss specific offers and tactics to begin this online conversation.

Below the fold, place 200-300 words of text to highlight who you are and what problems you treat or solutions you offer, as well as other services and benefits you can provide.

It's good to offer a free educational piece, which can be in the form of a video and/or text. You should also show any products that you have for sale.

The next thing to consider is the color that accents your website. Oddly enough, every industry seems to have its own colors. And, as you know, certain colors have certain subconscious implications. The typical color for medical websites is some shade of blue, which is the color most associated with trust.

WEBSITE CREATION

With free website platforms such as WordPress (WP) and millions of pre-designed and flexible templates, creating a website has never been easier. WordPress started as a blog platform but is now often used as an entire website and content management platform. The WP platform is extremely intuitive and easy to use. There are tools called plug-ins that add functionality to WP. Plug-ins transform this handy blog platform into a robust website platform that can handle millions of visitors and thousands of functions. With some effort, you can create your own website at a very nominal cost.

With that being said, unless you have experience in web design and web architecture, you should never design your own site. I can't overemphasize the concepts of architecture and process flow. Everything on your website should be strategic; there must be a reason for putting an icon in one area and not another. The more simple, clean, organized, easy to navigate and compelling your site is, the more likely a person will opt-in and become a future patient.

On the other hand, if a person visiting your site begins to fumble around, gets lost or even slightly confused, they will leave. You only have a few seconds to engage someone. The more time and thought you devote to the first few seconds a user 's experience on your website the better.

You might have an offer from one of your kids or their friends to build a site for you for a modest price of a few hundred dollars. This isn't a bad starting point to get something up quickly, but don't let it be your stopping point. There are global resources for finding designers and programmers who build solid sites for reasonable fees. (See the Resources section in the Appendix).

You may openly admit your ignorance about web design and go straight to finding an expert to create your new site, for thousands of dollars. But, he or she may be completely unfamiliar with the medical industry. Your new site might look great (to you), since you gave some direction to a creative web professional catering to *your* idea about what looks good. If possible, work with someone who has some experience producing high-quality medical websites – it can often make a big difference.

Now that the basic structure of your website has been discussed, let's look at additional tools and components that will add to both your visitors' and your own experience of your medical website.

MEDICAL WEBSITE MAINTENANCE

In the not-too-distant past, a simple website could be developed and forgotten ("Just set it and forget it!"). Times have changed, as websites have become more complex and interactive, especially with video and blogs. This means someone has to maintain the website to some extent. Technology changes pretty quickly these days in terms of the various features, tools and plug-ins that can be added to a website. Plug-ins cover a wide area of functionality and can be used to provide benefit to both your visitors and to you, the owner. For example, suppose a plug-in became available for your website that allowed people to schedule their own appointments online. You might want this integrated, and you'll want the same person who built your site to add this feature.

Or, you might want to add a plug-in that monitors your traffic and tells you where your visitors are coming from. This type of monitoring is getting more sophisticated all the time and is absolutely essential to understanding how effectively your marketing dollars are working.

With thousands of plug-ins, you are bound to become overwhelmed. That's natural. With a clear goal in mind and a blueprint for your online presence, your team will be able to design a perfect platform that can do everything except perform a procedure.

If you are in private practice and want to stay in private practice, you are going to have to get involved with some effective and efficient marketing practices, as it is now clear that you are competing with the hospital-owned practices.

ACTION STEPS

1. Evaluate your website from the point of view of solving a problem for someone, the ease of navigation and how easy it is to find your contact information.

2. See if your site immediately starts to provide a solution to a problem. Do you use a video to do this?

3. Choose a website designer/developer who is a professional and can help with placement and maintenance of the important components of a medical website and modify it when necessary.

In the next section, we will discover what education-based marketing is and how it can work for your medical practice.

CHAPTER TWO

MEDICAL WEBSITE COMPONENTS

Just like medicine, a website is a complex and constantly evolving entity. Fortunately, establishing the fundamentals is simple.

TRUE MARKETING IS EDUCATION

I cannot remember a time in my career when there has not been a dark cloud hanging over the concept of advertising or marketing in the medical field. Perhaps like you, I felt uncomfortable with the word "marketing" as a medical professional. To me, marketing represented the "Sham-Wow" infomercial. "I can never *market* my practice. What will people think?" "I shouldn't have to market my practice if I'm really good."

Has marketing become a slimy, four-letter word like "sales?" (Okay, that was five letters, but you get the idea.) As medical professionals, most of us have very little understanding of what good or proper marketing is. Furthermore, with a confusing array of terms like direct response, branding, client engagement and hundreds of other buzz words, it's easy to become confused and even annoyed. In the end, many dismiss that our profession should engage in marketing at all. Marketers don't get initials after their names. They didn't intern or train for years on four hours of sleep. We earned those initials and to engage in marketing is… well, crass. Unfortunately, the avoidance of good marketing has left the practice of medicine vulnerable to the pressures of insurance companies and the government.

You will always be a doctor but, in order to keep your practice healthy and your balance sheet out of the trauma center, we need to add education-based marketing to your background.

Don't think for a minute that marketing within the medical community hasn't been going on for decades; it has.

Medical marketing has been happening all around us, in a manner that we all considered acceptable. It's been a mainstay at conferences, presentations, contract care of sports teams and courses for allied health professionals. Every time you see a Prilosec commercial or open a magazine, medical marketing is happening. We see commercials branding hospitals, cancer clinics, cosmetic surgery and nasal spray. Medical marketing is everywhere.

These acceptable pathways of marketing all have one thing in common, and it is the common denominator of all good marketing: education.

When marketers of any product lead with relevant information and education, the perception of being "sold" isn't apparent. With education as the cornerstone of our practice, we should be comfortable hearing that education is the foundation of good marketing. In order to embrace education-based marketing for your practice, reflect upon how education *built* your practice. Recalling the hours of study, exams and practical experience you received to become a doctor and considering what you do for a living, you are more than a healer. You already are an educator.

We spend a large percentage of time in the office asking our patients questions, pulling from our education and applying a diagnosis. We bring our skills and experience to their lives. We suggest lifestyle changes and exercises to assist our patients in getting better. We share our knowledge and ourselves.

We heal through education.

Why limit ourselves to educating patients only in the office? Why not try to educate them before they see us? This type of "education in advance" is amazingly effective as a tool to speed up our diagnosis. This approach has a three-pronged benefit: respectable marketing, qualified referrals and the generation of trust and authority. With a properly-constructed website and educational tools, you will be able to educate in advance, so you can maintain your patient flow and begin to increase your volume if desired.

Skeptically, one may ask, "Why talk about information that is readily available on the Internet?" While 99 percent of the information you package and even sell may already be online for free, helping your patients navigate the truth in an ocean of conflicting information has major value. Packaging and positioning the information is not just a great idea, it's required. Additionally, it happens to be quite lucrative.

With over 644 million websites on the Internet, it is impossible *not* to be confused. Your patients probably don't know the difference between a double-blind study done by one researcher and another done by an offshore pharmaceutical company. Your patients desperately want and need the truth. For many physicians, the scientific research and knowledge gained has become so second nature, we intuitively know what solid information is and what is B.S.

Your patients don't have the luxury of your experience. They need and want your perspective.

Give it to them. Later on, I'll show you how to monetize this education effortlessly. Before that, however, we need to teach patients how to learn.

EDUCATING IN ADVANCE

This concept of educating in advance lends itself very well to a proper medical website and an online engagement system. The education you will be providing will be of high value to your prospective patient. There are three critical reasons your website should immediately provide authentic value.

CREDIBILITY

Provide value in the form of information or education for someone who has a problem you may be able to solve. When someone visits your website looking for answers, giving them a reason to *stay* on your website increases your credibility and smoothly transitions them to becoming a future patient or client. You are more than simply the authority – you are the credible expert.

RELATIONSHIP

Your doctor-patient relationship begins before you actually meet. A website visitor who is properly educated gets to know you a little. Provided you do this in a personal style, your visitors can get a glimpse of your personality. You can use engagement tools such as social media, video and curated content, to start to be seen as the trusted authority who may be able to solve their problems. Before someone can trust you, they need to get to know you. Beginning this relationship virtually by leading with a giving hand bodes well for both you and them.

CHOICE

Give your website visitors a reason to choose you as their doctor. If the tables were reversed, you would certainly choose someone who you knew a little (and hopefully liked), more than you would choose someone of whom you had no knowledge. Your chances of being chosen as their primary doctor or specialist increase tremendously when you selflessly provide some free information that can potentially solve problems.

With the blueprint we provide to our members and tutorials any office manager can follow, you have the opportunity to take advantage of website and video technology that either didn't exist before or was too expensive for the average medical practitioner to employ. You can now start to educate people and begin a relationship with them before they actually come into contact with you. You become the obvious choice for prospective patients.

VIDEO IS A MUST

Properly done, video is one of the most dynamic and interpersonal tools now within reach of any physician/marketer. Educating and building a relationship using this visual medium has been proven by TV and the film industry for decades and, until recently, was out of reach for small- and medium-sized businesses.

Before the Internet, CNN and other cable TV upstarts made a dent in the monopoly of CBS, NBC and ABC.

YouTube and other on-demand services have decreased broadcast TV viewing by half in the past few years. This trend has not destroyed broadcast TV, but it has permanently opened up our computers to content. Recently, Cisco Systems announced a complete revamping of its product line (translation: the technology that runs the Internet) to handle massive amounts of video traffic. There is a massive shift in how we absorb information. On-line video is a megatrend, and it's here to stay.

What this means to you is that, with a simple camera (or your smartphone) you can and should "star" on your own medical practice website. Before you think you have to act or be more presentable, relax. It's actually better not to be too slick. As every smartphone, PC and tablet has become a personal recording studio, people have become accustomed to images, trainings and news delivered in a more casual manner.

Think of the power of film to create images of people and things for us to remember. You've used visual aids as a doctor for years. We are visual creatures and, by combining well-positioned textual content with video, you catapult your efficacy as a physician-educator miles ahead of anyone else.

You don't need video everywhere but, for starters, you should have a video on the landing page of your website.

There is no question that we are bombarded from morning to night with attempts to get our attention. These attempts come from everywhere: family, friends, email, cell phones, texting, sales reps, radio, TV, billboards, newspapers and magazines ad nauseam. These intrusions run the gamut from welcomed to disliked; if we aren't familiar with the source, it better be highly engaging to get and keep our attention.

It's easy to click away.

Broadcast marketing is largely based on interrupting our brain patterns. We watch a soap opera or sports game and the commercials are interrupting our train of thought.

A typical medical website is not interrupting anything.

There is no disputing that the human mind is wired to focus on movement, as opposed to something that is static. Perhaps that hints at the power of video and why it has become the dominant media source within a short time after its introduction. We are genetically hardwired to watch something moving; if there is accompanying sound, so much the better. Our natural tendency to watch movement and listen to sound is related to our survival instincts and is deeply engrained in our DNA, even when survival is not an issue.

One interesting feature of the human brain is its ability to quickly adapt to new things and make a new standard. This was obvious when "talkies" replaced silent film in the 1920s or when TV replaced radio in the 1950s. We only have to look at the popularity of YouTube to see the dominant place that video has in the media.

YouTube is not just about watching "cats fighting in the driveway" and other entertaining (but not serious) videos. This media platform is maturing rapidly in terms of content and popularity. In July 2011, YouTube became more popular as a search engine than its parent/partner Google. Placing your education-based content on YouTube is expected from an ever-increasing audience of sophisticated patients. To avoid it is M2D... medical marketing death.

Personally, I like to read, so it can be hard for me to believe that video is so tremendously popular. There is no disputing the popularity of YouTube, however: it is the largest video platform in the world.

Below is a brief overview to get you started. For a detailed blueprint and tutorial, visit my membership program at www.MedicalWebsiteAcademy.com.

First of all, if you are not using video and are wondering where to start, think Apple products.

One reason Apple products are so insanely popular is because they are integrated. When you shoot a high-definition video with your iPhone, it is not much different than the interface on your iPad. Even all laptop and desktop models come with crystal-clear video capture that can record you sharing an idea or health tip.

If being on camera is not your style but you still want to have some video, you can use the built-in program called Keynote, which is Apple's easy-to-use version of Microsoft's PowerPoint program. Create a slide show, and use your own voice to narrate it. If you plug in a high-quality microphone, you can give a high-quality audio presentation of the Keynote slides. You can easily insert video clips into the Keynote slides for a more stimulating presentation. Click through your slides while recording your commentary.

Next, upload your presentation to YouTube. You can then place this video on the landing page of your website. What is the cost for this?

Zip. Zero. Nilch. Nada. Provided you have a computer or a smartphone (which don't *have* to be Apple products), every step of this system is 100 percent free.

Once your video is up on YouTube, you can send the "embed code" of the video to your web designer. The embed code identifies the "address" of your video; just copy and paste the code into an email, and send it to him or her. If that is outside your comfort zone, send your web designer a link to your YouTube channel and he or she can easily copy and paste the code. The web designer will then create a link on your webpage that connects to the video.

Easy-peasy.

People looking at your website are seeking information to solve a problem; they want to know what you have to say. First impressions are important, so use a video to say something of value, and let it come from your heart. Our profession is being bombarded with negative and impersonal images, sales pitches and ads for drugs. The more you bring the human touch and your personality to your video, the better. Be yourself.

Video placement on your website is very important. Your introductory video should be one of the first things that someone sees on your site. It should be located on your landing page so that it is visible without anyone scrolling up or down (as previously mentioned, what we call "above the fold").

Use the video to introduce yourself and immediately start to add value by educating the visitor. Remember, they are trying to solve medical problems and hope that you have the answers. Talk like you are speaking to your best friend. Smile, relax and be brief. Website visitors have the attention span of a gnat, so get to the point immediately.

It is a fact that people like to perceive information through their preferred sense. In other words, some people learn best by listening, others like to read text and some like to view a video to get information. Since you don't know how the person viewing your website will want your information delivered, provide a mixture of all three formats (text, audio and video) to convey your information. In other words, use video with audio and a textual summary to convey your message. For starters, it doesn't matter if you film yourself or narrate a Keynote/PowerPoint presentation. Don't get hung up on the minutia about the lighting or what you should wear. The point is to create the video and get it up on your website. The information you provide will begin to attract people who resonate with you and your point of view.

As you get feedback and experience, you will update and upgrade your video and presentation skills. Unlike your printed brochures from the past, your website and videos are dynamic and can be changed instantly and for little to almost no cost.

GIVE SOMETHING EDUCATIONAL AWAY

There is another way to give value and provide education for someone looking at your website. Keep in mind, some content may be too lengthy or rich to deliver in a short blog post or in a two-minute audio/video clip. For your more robust educational content, use what is called a "white paper," "ethical bribe" or "freebie." Create an educational piece that can be downloaded directly from your site in the form of a PDF (portable document format). This type of document is in text format and can also include images. It can be something as simple as a "Consumer Awareness Guide" that describes the features and benefits of something you are offering or doing in your practice. This document is simply created in Microsoft Word and saved as a PDF. If the situation warrants, you can even publish this as a short electronic book (ebook) that visitors can download on your site or on Amazon.

When you are satisfied with the document, send it to your web designer in an email attachment so he or she can integrate it. Your web designer can place a small picture of your "Free Consumer Awareness Guide" (always use visually stimulating pictures when possible) on your landing page, along with an opt-in form. When someone fills out the opt-in form (as simple as entering their name and email address), your PDF will immediately be sent to their email address, where they can download and read it. Of course, always put your name and contact information on the front of the PDF and at the end, and be sure to tell the prospective patient to call your office for more information.

After they get the PDF in their email, you should also send an automated follow-up email, thanking the person for their inquiry and interest. This could also be followed by a friendly email a few days later asking if they have additional questions. This entire sequence is presented in a step-by-step fashion, complete with a video tutorial at www.MedicalWebsiteAcademy.com.

NEWSLETTERS

Another compelling way to educate and engage your patients is with a newsletter. A newsletter is generally given away on a timed schedule and allows you to stay in touch with someone and create a relationship. Sometimes newsletters actually relate to the news. Any updates on new medicines, insurance, etc., could be noteworthy items your patients care about.

In most cases, however, the newsletter should contain in-depth information that is "evergreen" and relevant regardless of the news cycle. This way, as new subscribers continue to sign up, the content they receive is not outdated.

There are dozens of strategies concerning newsletter engagement. You must consider the demographics and psychographics of your audience, length and relevance; then, determine a palatable balance between providing quality content and marketing.

A newsletter can be created for potential patients or potential referral sources. *It is essential to know where your patients come from at all times!* A patient who finds me on the Internet may come to see me if he or she likes my content. He or she may refer a friend if the experience with me is pleasurable. On the other hand, if I can educate a professional who sees a lot of patients who might be referred to me, it could be even better for my bottom line.

You may have two separate engagement tools: one for patients and one for referral sources.

Consider which professionals might possibly refer to you their patients or clients. In my case, as an endoscopic spinal surgeon, there are three groups of professionals that might want to refer me. These three groups are pain management doctors, chiropractors and physical therapists. Each group has a slightly different reason as to why they might refer patients to me, but each group is constantly in contact with the kind of patients I can help.

When contemplating your newsletter(s), it will be a daunting thought that you have to create all of that content! By identifying your referral sources or "power partners," you not only have an established source of prospective subscribers but guest writers as well.

Like all established editors of any magazine, having others publish their content is immensely easier than writing it all yourself. You can put in your own "Editor's Corner" article if you wish, but since the newsletter comes from your office, the reader will always identify you as the source.

I provide a newsletter to each group, sending out a new post every four to six weeks. See www.Endoscopicspinenewsletter. com and www.DCNewsletter.com for examples.

These newsletters offer some periodic education that builds a relationship between possible referral sources and me.

Another advantage to a newsletter is that a patient or doctor will give you his or her name and email (opting in) in exchange for the newsletter. The names and email addresses that you acquire are the beginning of building your "list" or "tribe." We will talk more about the strategy and tactics of building your list in a moment.

If you publish a topic that is popular and your content is of high enough value, you have the possibility of charging a monthly subscription fee for your newsletter. Subscription income is extremely exciting. People get used to subscriptions once the value is established and the subscriber treats the information as essential. Like cable, cellular or your financial newsletter, a monthly fee can be a very reasonable exchange provided that you deliver content that meets or exceeds your chosen price point.

With a few hundred or even a thousand subscribers (not a large number) it doesn't take much to see that being a publisher can add significantly to your bottom line. The best part is that you are sharing information that you normally share anyway. The difference is only how you package and position the content. Instead of talking to one patient, you package your information (and the knowledge of others) into a readable and valuable newsletter.

WHY YOU NEED A BLOG

It really took quite a long time for me to personally understand the use of a blog on a medical website. I am definitely not an exceptional writer and have never considered myself prolific in terms of writing information pieces. However, when I began to grasp the benefits of a blog, I got serious about it.

You don't need to write the next New England Journal of Medicine article. Lay people don't read those, anyway. In fact, the more casual and conversational you are in your blog the better.

A blog (short for "web log") is a personal and intimate communication platform between you and a reader. It should be designed and written as though you are speaking to one person. Often, bloggers get caught up in their list and how many subscribers they have. Groups don't read blogs. Individuals do. Blogs are easy to write when you consider the perspective that you are simply talking to a prospective patient.

You do it every day, anyway. With a blog, it's just in writing or video.

So what is a blog? It's an informational section of your website where you regularly write about a particular topic or area of interest. Your entries are usually arranged in chronological order, with the most recent "post" at the top of the main blog page and older entries towards the bottom.

Your blog should be integrated into your website and will typically be found by clicking a "Blog" tab or link on your homepage or landing page. Blog posts are created from text, video, audio or a combination of media. Once your piece has been created, you or your web designer can upload it to your blog. Many bloggers compile a dozen or more posts at a time and load them into their blog system. The system can automatically publish these posts three or four times per week (or at any frequency you desire). This enables you to publish a consistent stream of content on your website.

This consistent stream of content shows the search engines that your site is active and has valuable information. Pre-loading a week or two worth of posts is an efficient use of your time and no one will ever know that you pre-loaded your batch of posts.

Your blog serves a multitude of purposes, including:

1. Creating searchable keywords in the title and content.

2. Developing relationships with people who want to know what you think about a certain topic.

3. Adding new information to your website that helps with your Google ranking.

4. Establishing your brand and credibility.

5. Doing a review on a product or supplement.

6. Creating a sales page to sell a product or supplement.

A blog is social in nature and can help you to create a fan base. Your blog is a place for you to "talk" (whether by video and/or text) about something interesting or pertinent to the people visiting your website. In some cases, a visitor may be embarrassed to discuss a certain topic in person. Your blog gives him or her a chance to ask you anything, anonymously. By asking for reader comments and questions when you post, you transform a one-way communication platform into a conversation.

The Internet search engines "crawl" your blog, so using plenty of keywords that relate to your services is very important when you write your blog posts. If you are skillful about this, your blog posts may show up on the organic (nonpaid) left side of a Google search results page, when someone searches for a keyword you've referenced. If you show up in the search results, someone may then click on your link and will be taken directly to your blog.

Blogging Tip:

Interview someone in your field who can lend further insight on your topic. By adding their credibility to your own, you double your effectiveness for half the work.

Each blog post is something you have created in text (usually 500–750 words) and/or video. It's also a great idea to transcribe your videos and enter them as an additional component to your blog post. Title your blog post using keywords that the search engines are likely to pick up. For example, as of this writing, someone searching Google for "cervical foraminal stenosis" will see a video from my blog, on the front page of Google. How cool is that?

Using "content-rich" words in your blog post's title or first few sentences will connect you with people looking for your services and expertise. Your blog posts will provide you exposure on the search engines like Google or Bing, for free. At the end of a blog post, invite your readers to contact you and to leave their comments and questions.

CREATING BLOG CONTENT

IDEAS FOR BLOG POSTS

1. Create your own story, observations or information on a relvant topic in text, video or Keynote/PowerPoint presentation.

2. Paraphrase a recent journal article of interest (with credit or reference to the author, of course).

3. Interview someone of interest in your field (the person interviewed will appreciate the additional exposure).

STEPS TO CREATING A BLOG POST

1. Write a 500–700 word article with unique, interesting and keyword-rich content, or shoot a short two- to six-minute video. Content is king, and you can transcribe your video and post the text separately for double the effectiveness.

2. Title the piece with keyword-rich words that your audience might search for. Use keywords and phrases that are designed to attract the search engines.

3. Put your website and any other contact information toward the bottom of the piece.

4. Proofread it. While casual conversation is critical to developing a relationship online, don't avoid having a live person visually proof your post.

5. Post it. Submit the piece to your web designer or post it yourself through the admin portal he or she will provide to you.

6. Done. If search engines find and like your content, you may find yourself on the front page of Google on the trusted, organic side of the page...for free!

Tip

We will talk about SEO (search engine optimization) a little later, but one tip I learned recently was to give my "unique" blog post to my SEO guy before publishing it to my blog. He can sometimes have it posted on someone else's specialty blog (that somehow relates to me or my post topic) as a unique piece of content.

If your post is published to your own blog first, it is no longer considered unique (and other people generally want unique content to post, not something you've already published)! Once your post is up on someone else's site, you may get discovered more readily and gain more traffic and recognition as you become a trusted authority. Once the unique piece has gotten on to someone else's site, you can then put it up on your own. By submitting your article to someone else first, you get a lot more potential exposure to his or her readers, who might then be directed back to you.

ACTION STEPS

1. Think about your landing page in terms of educational value to the viewer. Focus on a common problem and how you can solve it. Offer education, value and downloadable information pieces on your landing page. Remember that "value" may be your simple solution to a complex problem.

2. Video is a must on your landing page.

3. Use the video to "educate in advance" and start a relationship.

4. You can be a trusted authority before someone meets you.

5. Create items with educational value to give away (awareness guide or newsletter).

6. Have a blog and update it at least monthly.

In the next chapter, we will talk about the ways to drive more-visitors (also called "traffic") to your website.

CHAPTER THREE

ACQUIRING NEW CUSTOMERS

Most physicians don't realize their education can be shared and monetized beyond their town, county, state and country. Your perspective and skills are needed by the world, and people are willing to pay you for it.

You have a website populated with your content. You've recorded a few videos and blogged for a week or two to get com- fortable. There is an opt-in form and an automated email message set up when someone clicks on your free ebook or report. Everything is functional, relevant and ready. But you have one small problem: nobody knows where to find you.

You need traffic. The word traffic means website visitors. There are only a few basic strategies (but hundreds of tactics) to acquire visitors. Let's first cover the basics:

1. Paid traffic. There are thousands of ad placement oppor- tunities to advertise your website. From Google, Facebook and hundreds of media networks that can target your list- ing, paid traffic is a topic worthy of an entire book.

2. Organic traffic. When people search for something, they generally go to Google, Yahoo, or Bing. Behind the scenes at these search engine companies, a highly secret algorithm determines how millions of websites are ranked in the search engine results.

In this book, we will focus mostly on organic traffic, as the lessons for education-based search engine optimization (SEO) are ample.

The underlying forces that drive traffic are keywords - the spe- cific words or phrases that potential patients type into a search en- gine when they're looking for your product or service (i.e. "ortho- pedic surgeon newport beach, ca"). What you think those words or phrases are and what they really are can be two very different stories indeed.

NOTE: Keywords and their combinations are ranked by com- petition and relevancy. The more competition (more providers us- ing this word in their content) the more difficult it is to rank for that term. The lower the competition, the easier it is to rank...but lower ranking keywords are searched less.

Do you begin to see the challenge? With an infinite combination of words and phrases, your mind may spin when it comes to selecting keywords for which you wish to rank, when you begin to farm for Internet traffic.

There were certain topics to which I wanted to attract patients, and I would let my SEO consultants pick the appropriate keywords or phrases. Wow, did we come up with some different ideas!

We were looking at different reasons to choose a keyword or key phrase. They would be looking for low competition and the possibility of ranking high for that word or phrase, while I was looking to rank for a specific term that related to a very specific part of my practice. On more than one occasion, I found there was very little in common.

Furthermore, when well-established players have spent hundreds of thousands of dollars and years establishing their brand, they may dominate a keyword phrase you desire.

If you rank high on keywords that are not related to your expertise, it won't help you. If you are like me, you have limited amounts of time and money to spend on any aspect of your practice, particularly things that are unfamiliar or that other people are being paid to (or are supposed to) do. The simple fact is, you must assist a bit with your keyword search since it is the cornerstone of your efforts to drive traffic to your website.

This preliminary work to select the proper keywords and phrases doesn't cost anything except time. This time is generally a good investment because you can waste a lot of money if you decide to put the bulk of your resources into paid advertising on Google, Facebook or an ad network...targeting less-than-optimal keywords. You can't go into this arena thinking that you can just throw money at the process and it will work out. It won't. You need to be much more strategic, as the variables of search are about as easy and uncomplicated as predicting the weather (with the exception of San Diego).

Let's start with the obvious process that you have used countless times to find something on the Internet. Think of how you go through the process of finding something online; then, simply reverse-engineer the process.

Start by typing in a phrase or word, and see what comes up. Although you may feel that you already know what the most obvious keywords are, I have been surprised to find out that Google did not always agree with me. Keep in mind that Google runs the show here, so work with Google, and you will have more success.

Although there are some paid services that can do this for you, such as Keyword Spy, start with the free service Google has to help you identify commonly searched keywords and phrases. All you need is a Google AdWords account. Start by creating a new AdWords account by visiting https://adwords.google.com and clicking *Get started now*. The sign-up process differs depending on whether you already have a Google Account (in other words, if you use any other Google product, such as Gmail), or if you're new to Google.

Google wants you to know what the best keywords are for your business, so that you will use your AdWords account to target them with paid ads.

Once you have created your AdWords account and opened the site, you will see a tab on the top of the page that says "Tools and Analysis." Click this and then, click on "Keyword Tool." At the top, you can type any word and some further choices will come up; you can see how many local and global choices there are for such a keyword. In other words, you can see what people are typing in to find certain information on a certain topic.

This identification of correct keywords is *critical* to everything you are going to do to drive traffic. You can't spend too much time doing your research in this area.

Use these keywords in your URL when possible, in the header, tagline and on the landing page (of your website), in the title of your blog, and in the first few sentences of your blog posts or your paid ads. When someone types in words and searches, the idea is that the search engine will reference your website, landing page or blog (where you have the keywords throughout text).

KEEPING TRACK

After investing your precious resources, money and time into building your website, it is important to track how it is functioning. When people call your office, your admin should ask how they found you and what they were searching for. Was it word-of-mouth, a referral source, YouTube, a newspaper ad or the Internet? This must be done and written down or put into a spreadsheet for every new person coming into a practice. For whatever reason, doing this simple task has been one of the most difficult things to convince employees to do and maintain. I have hired "marketing" people for high, five-digit salaries who didn't get this or follow through with it. It is now part of the job description for my people. This information is critical to help you know where to spend your money for promotion or to develop inroads to your business that currently don't exist.

If they found you online, ask what words they used "to search for you or your service," and write it down. Keep an index of the commonly-used keywords and phrases that you find. Someone must ask this question consistently; the answers are often not what you would think! When evaluating these keywords, the customer is always right – what they searched for is what they searched for. Their answers are critical to choosing the correct keywords, which you will then use to strategically place in your URL, header, blog and ads.

You can make a real science of this but only if the data is collected. The medical profession just doesn't have enough money sloshing around in a practice to be wasting money with questionable marketing techniques. Collect the data.

It's also common to spend thousands of dollars on questionable advertising or marketing and not buy lunch for the office staff of the doctor who sends you referrals on a consistent basis; common, but not smart! Market or die, as I like to say...but do it the right way.

THE "SEARCH"

Once someone types a word or phrase into the search bar, a page of possible search results emerges. This is called the "front page" of Google, which is important because people don't usually search back past the first page or two. You want your site to show up in the first few pages, if not on the front page.

Notice how the page is divided. The search results on the right side are in colored boxes; these are paid ads. Someone has paid Google to place the ads there for you to see. Google, using their proprietary formula, determines the rank or placement of a paid ad. There are also some ads at the top of the page that have a highlighted background; these are paid ads as well.

The websites and references listed on the left side of the page below the highlighted ads are all nonpaid. The results listed here are called "organic" or "trusted" sources. You can't buy your way into this part, and that is why it is the "trusted" side. Instead, you must be ranked (by Google, Bing or Yahoo) to get here. This process of ranking is usually determined by the "freshness," relevancy and authority of the content referenced. The methods that Google uses to rank sites are proprietary, complex and multi-layered, so it can be a difficult task to figure out how you get on the first few pages. And, if Google makes changes to their algorithm, everything can change quickly.

This whole business of paid versus nonpaid advertising on the Internet is very interesting, because you really have to make a decision about your strategy to get people to your site.

In other words, do you want to attract people searching from the "paid" side (quickest results) or the "organic" or trusted side (slow and strategic)?

Although you may think that the organic side is free, you are going to pay money in either case, either to Google AdWords or to an SEO expert who can help place and link your content in a way that helps Google to recognize and rank you more favorably. There is also the cost of hiring a video person or someone to help you write fresh content, if you do not have the time or inclination. You should do a little of both paid and nonpaid.

BUY IT—GOOGLE, CPC, AND IMAGE ADS

Let's talk about Google paid ads first. The two types of ads are pay-per-click (PPC) and image ads. Let's talk about PPC first. Writing an ad campaign on the paid side will certainly be the quickest way to attract patients or clients.

Making an ad is not difficult; just choose some keywords or keyword phrases. Then, place the ad using the directions that Google provides. You can do this yourself, but I would enlist the help of an SEO specialist who can help craft a strategy before any money is spent.

Establish a budget with a limit (a budget is a necessity, especially with expensive keywords) and run the ad. You are now running a campaign.

Your ad will show up in the paid section of the search results page when someone types in the keyword or key phrase that you're targeting. When a person clicks your ad, they are taken to your website or the webpage linked to the ad. Google charges your account the amount it specifies in advance for each click.

Google AdWords is incredibly sophisticated and allows you to advertise to a certain country, state or city. Facebook advertising is even more sophisticated and can be directed to zip codes, books people have read, political affiliations...the works! Knowing your client is more important than you can possibly imagine.

Some keywords are expensive. With an expensive keyword, you can go through a thousand dollars pretty quickly. Whether you are a solo practitioner or large group, you will have to establish an advertising budget that you can manage and support on a consistent basis.

The "image ad" concept is a bit more obscure. When creating an image ad, you pay for your ad or an "image of your ad" to be shown on certain sites or pages that Google feels might be relevant to your keywords. Image ads are paid for by exposure, not by who clicks on the ad.

For example, if you are involved with a lap-band procedure, and you have an image ad campaign running, the network may display your ad on a webpage that talks about weight loss. Your ad will be shown on pages that Google considers relevant. The image ad may get clicked or not, but for every 1,000 times that it is shown, you get charged. There is no guarantee that anyone will click your ad. It is an inexpensive way to get exposure, but you have no control about where your ad will show up; Google determines that.

You can spend some time with the Google Analytics program in your AdWords account to see how your ad campaign is performing. You can check the number of people visiting, how long they stayed on your site, and how quickly your budget is depleted. The Analytics page can be found on the AdWords page under the "Campaigns" and "Tools and Analysis" tabs. A good SEO person will be invaluable here to help interpret what is going on.

"FREE" ADVERTISING

There are many ways to drive traffic to your site without paying Google, per se. The following strategy still requires an investment, and it will usually involve hiring an SEO person to implement the linking process between your website and other sources of content.

Establish your blog. You must have an active blog with links. You create the content for your blog, and your SEO person will create the links. A word of caution here: don't just buy thousands of links! This artificial way of looking more active than you really are will be severely penalized by Google when they figure it out. You will be penalized in terms of search ranking for whatever terms you were establishing links for. Be careful here. Google emphasizes being a trusted authority; buying links is not considered trustworthy.

Think of your blog site as the active or dynamic section of your website, where you talk about new things or ideas. Let's say that you are giving a lecture at a conference, and you can provide the web address to that conference. A link can be established between your blog and the conference, so any searches for the conference may result in a reference to your blog. If the conference website is a good one, they will have you listed as a speaker and provide your website address – that's another link back to your site.

What is the big deal about links? Google's algorithm looks at this kind of activity and sees it as relevant and authoritative. The greater the number of links to and from your website that get clicked, the more relevant Google thinks your content is. There is as much art as science to proper linking. Hiring a skilled SEO expert is a wise investment in this area.

A skilled SEO expert – one who has a recent track record of success – is about as important to your website's health as a new medical procedure that doubles the survival rates is to your patients. These are the people who are the experts in finding the best keywords (with your help), will write an ad and optimize the campaign for it, can use linking to great advantage and send out strategic press releases. All this is done to raise your ranking in areas where you want to be found. This person will also help to strategize, budget and manage a marketing campaign on Google or Facebook. Be honest and skip getting overwhelmed; you are too busy to do a good job in this department. Outsource it.

The SEO expert can also be of great help if a reputation management situation crops up. Sociopaths represent five percent of the population, and if one hones in on you on the Internet, he or she can post negative information instantly and prolifically. In many cases, this tarnishing of your reputation can be worse than a frivolous lawsuit. In the case of a lawsuit, there is a beginning and an end, with a system in place to adjudicate. The Internet still resembles the Wild West in some ways. Retaining a good SEO expert can be more valuable than a lawyer (and will cost a lot less).

Sociopaths or not, ensure that your blog posts allow and encourage visitor comments. Commenting is "activity" and should be sought out. Use a Facebook "comment box" inserted by your web designer. If a visitor leaves a comment in this box, it will not only show up on your blog post, it will also post their comment to their Facebook timeline. This will essentially link your blog to Facebook, which increases your SEO, authority and reach.

Another traffic driver is Google's video site, YouTube (yep, they own it now). Start by setting up a channel that is associated with a Gmail address. Name the channel and then start uploading video content about your particular topic. In the video and tags, name your website "for more information contact us at [your website]…" this acts as a link back to your website. In my case, I have two YouTube channels, Drtonymork and Endoscopicspine.

You should feature your videos on your blog, which you or your web designer can embed into your blog posts.

When you upload your videos to YouTube, have the audio portion transcribed and post the text to your blog as well. By adding a variety of media, you'll appeal to a greater number of viewers.

RECAP

At this point you have created a website with value. You have established a budget for driving organic and paid traffic, and you are about to hire an SEO expert.

Before you pull out your checkbook, examine your focus and what you want to accomplish with the money you spend to drive traffic to your website. The more focused you are about what you offer, the more satisfied you will be with who you are attracting to your practice. An in-depth analysis of your focus will save you thousands with your marketing dollars, whether you pay for ads or for the SEO (or both). It will also make this whole process a lot more fun.

For many of you, this will be your first endeavor into this medium, and you will go much farther and faster if you take a strategic approach. Consider the problems patients have and how you can sincerely attract these folks to your practice. Focus on them.

Frankly, you already do plenty of things that don't turn you on. Use this opportunity (building your medical website) to figure out what is energizing and exciting to you, when it comes to being involved with the online aspect of your practice. The Internet will bring you what you want, if you use it properly. The more content-oriented you are, the more fun and excitement you will have to share with your prospective patients – all while truly helping them with your experience and expertise.

ACTION STEPS

1. Open a Google AdWords account.

2. Use the Google Keyword Tool to start finding the words
   and phrases that people are using when they search for
   your services, products and/or specialty.

3. Put the keywords from Step 2 into your website URL, header, tags and blog posts.

4. The person answering your phone is the most important
   per- son in your office next to you, as he or she is the first
   point of contact for a patient or client. This same person
   must write down where your patients are coming from,
   how they found you and what keywords they used.

5. Begin to employ the services of a good SEO expert to help
   draw up a both a budget and a strategy for increasing both
   paid and nonpaid traffic to your website.

6. You must have a blog that you post to at least once a month.

7. Start thinking about short three- to five-minute videos to
   start shooting, and consider looking for a video person to
   shoot and edit. (An easy place to look is for people who
   film weddings)

Not to overwhelm you, but there is more – much more – about
building this new empire. Keep in mind, you can outsource 90
percent of all this, and, with a clear, step-by-step plan in place,
much of the work is done only once.

To give you some perspective, in the next chapter we will talk
about creating a list and my personal, $1.8 million mistake.

CHAPTER FOUR

MY $1.8 MILLION MISTAKE

When it comes to your medical website, the power of your list and the intimacy it involves can be expanded by a factor of 10X or even maybe 100X.

When I practiced in Florida, our office website would routinely get 10,000 visitors a month, month after month. This Internet traffic went on for years.

"So what?" you may ask. "What is the big deal, Tony?"

At the time, I didn't know what the big deal was either. I didn't understood what a list was...or what the power of such a thing is.

In retrospect, the 10,000 visitors a month from 2000–2010 turned out to be the single largest missed opportunity for me in the past twenty years. Are you still wondering what I'm talking about?

Consider your current list. You have a list of patients who have come to know you over the years. These people are not merely numbers in your database. They are people whom you have healed, counseled and worked with. These are people who have (perhaps through their insurance carriers) paid for the roof over your head, the car in your garage and your kids' braces. Your list of patients, past and present, like that of many physicians, may be in the hundreds or thousands.

It is that list, cultivated over the years, that has precluded you from having to market.

When it comes to your medical website, the power of your list and the intimacy it involves can be expanded by a factor of 10X or even maybe 100X.

In many cases, online traffic that converts to repeat visitors can be monetized. Successful newsletter publishers routinely boast $0.50 to $2.50 per name per MONTH of revenue.

In the world of Internet marketing, the average product sells for $47. Wise marketers always calculate the lifetime value (what a person will spend with you over their lifetime) with the cost to acquire that name. With a list of 10,000 people and an average monthly income of $1, a healthy $10,000-per-month income can be generated by simply offering a newsletter, supplements, reports—or even affiliate products on occasion—to your list.

In the world of medicine, the lifetime value of a name on a list can be worth more than $47…much more.

Depending on your specialty, an engaged name on your list can be worth a considerable amount. I personally know many cosmetic surgeons who calculate their database value not simply on the procedures they deliver, but the referrals they garner from their list. The value is almost incalculable.

HOW DO YOU CREATE A LIST?

A list is what is generated when someone visits a website and enters their name and email address. The name of the person is collected and stored by an autoresponder system.

This is very important for two reasons:

1. This group of people has actively sought you out to solve problems they have, for which you might have an answer.

2. They have given you a way to keep in touch with them.

I am sure you are beginning to see why such a list is so important. In my case, by not having a list, I lost out on any way to stay in touch with about 1.2 million people who had a specific problem (neck or back pain) and felt that I might be able to solve it. This group of people found me with no advertising cost to me!

As you can fathom, my $1.8 million mistake was probably much greater than $1.8 million.

If I had a list of the people who had found me on the Internet, I could have stayed in contact with them to see, build a relationship and answer further questions. Would everyone have become my patient? Not likely. However, with 10,000 visitors per month, rest assured, we would have been able to easily increase our practice tenfold in those years. Ouch.

It would have been great to let these folks know that I had

changed locations in 2011, instead of making them have to find me again, even if they could remember my name. I don't know the averages for each specialty, but the average orthopedic surgeon will move three times in his career. Wouldn't it be nice to let your patients know where you are?

Much more significant was the fact that in 2012, I created an information product about neck and back pain that could have helped a lot of these people. Without a list, I had no idea who they were.

The information product I created (comprised of a manual, DVD and CD) sells for $147. A lot of those people might have purchased this product from me, if they knew that I had it!

Having a list would have allowed me to send an email about my product to this problem-specific group of people, without spending a penny for advertising! Yikes, what a missed opportunity.

Think of that: even if 1 percent of the 1.2 million people bought my back pain relief product for $147, we are talking over $1.7 million!

The revenue potential of your list, in a few short months, can outperform any retirement you've taken years to build.

WHAT IS A LIST?

What makes up a list? A list is made up of 1) names of people and 2) their email addresses (may also include a phone number). How does one create a list? The process in which the person gives you a name and email address occurs in a little box on your website called an opt-in form, which includes fields for them to enter their information and then submit it. This opt-in form is connected to an autoresponder, (an automated feature in an email marketing system or platform) which stores the information in a list and is also set up to automatically send an email to them with something like a thank you message, a special report or a video. There are email marketing platforms that handle all technical aspects of this area. There are hundreds of options, but a few dominant brands serve most successful companies.

These include AWeber, iContact, Mailchimp and Constant Contact. Each has different pricing and the features vary somewhat.

Your list is generated by the opt-in form and autoresponder, which should be installed on your website by your website designer. The autoresponder system will allow you to contact people; they can also unsubscribe if they no longer wish to hear from you.

WHY WOULD SOMEONE GIVE YOU HIS OR HER CONTACT INFORMATION?

People will give you their name and email address if you have something they want and are willing to trade their email address for it.

Initially, you have given them an introduction to your service with some text or a short video that creates interest and starts to solve their problem. In other words, you are beginning to offer something of value to the person who has a specific problem. The introduction will then promise something of more substance (referred to as a "value piece" or "ethical bribe") in exchange for contact information.

For example, the introductory video on your homepage or landing page might end with "If you would like to know more..." or "If you would like to receive this ebook, or get a monthly subscription I created, just submit your name and email address and you will receive it (in your email) right away." You must initially get people interested in your promise or solution, and then trade your value piece for their name and email.

You must give before you receive.

The sequence proceeds in the following manner:

1. A person is "driven" to or finds your site.

2. They watch a short video or read something of interest and value that begins to help solve their problem.

3. Then you offer them something of additional and more comprehensive value if they will give you their name and email address.

4. They "opt-in" by entering their name and email address in the opt-in form(s) on your website.

5. Once they opt-in, their information is saved by an autoresponder system that automatically sends them whatever value piece you promised and a "thank you." You now have begun to form a list with the names and email addresses that are collected and stored by the autoresponder system.

Any email address the autoresponder system collects can now be used to contact that person again for a variety of reasons. For example, ask them if there is anything further you can do for them. Offer a free or discounted evaluation, additional value pieces (such as new research in your area of expertise), new services, a membership, a newsletter or something that you have for sale. Don't worry about being a "bother." At the bottom of any email communications sent from the autoresponder system, there is a place to unsubscribe. If people don't want to hear from you further, all they do is hit the "unsubscribe" button, and they are off your list.

RECOMMENDATIONS

1. Think strategically about the solutions you offer to the problems people have when they visit your website.

2. Start to offer these solutions in video or text.

3. Create a "value piece" that you can give to people in exchange for their name and email address.

4. Ask your web designer to add an opt-in form to your landing page that is connected to an autoresponder system that you have selected.

5. Ask your web designer to connect your value piece to the autoresponder, so that once someone opts in, they will get the value piece immediately in their email inbox.

6. Ask your web designer to follow the value piece with a "thank you" message.

NOTE: Every Internet marketer needs to follow the CAN SPAM Act of 2003, a law passed in Congress that sets rules for marketers and businesses who use email marketing. The law requires all commercial email to include the business's postal address, unsubscribe option, and the option for subscribers to choose what kinds of email they wish to receive. The Act also prohibits any misleading content including subjects, senders, messages and graphics.

CHAPTER FIVE

USE YOUR WEBSITE TO GENERATE SALES

Your experiences, circumstances and stories have tremendous value. Value that can and should be monetized. Your medical website can do more than pay for itself—it can pay you for a lifetime.

You are an expert.

Chances are you have special knowledge or a special program to help people with a certain problem. The Internet gives you a way to establish your expertise in a particular area and possibly help people further by offering them some sort of information product. The information product could be in text format (like a manual or ebook) in a video format or may also come in the form of a subscription membership. Properly packaged and presented, you may have something worth selling.

Many people have the misconception that everything is already on the the Internet and that there is no need for further information, let alone a way to charge for it!

The fallacy here is that most experts take their knowledge for granted. Additionally, your natural ability to synthesize this material and make some sense of it has tremendous value. As we mentioned earlier, your perspective, positioning and packaging of your specialized knowledge gives people what the truly want: a distilled, trusted solution to their problem.

People need and are willing to pay you to distill your large body of knowledge and have your information refined into an easy-to-understand solution to their problem. In the medical field, these possibilities are endless. If your specialty is allergies, then your knowledge of allergies as it applies to food choices, lifestyle, biology, pharmacology or any other vertical topic is marketable. You can create, publish, and market inside these verticals to solidify your relationship with your list.

The Internet gives you a vehicle to attract people to your website and provide a possible solution. There are many situations where you can create and sell an information product via your website that earns you a small royalty. While this may not seem as lucrative as a medical procedure, consider the benefits:

1. Your information products are evergreen. You create them once and resell them over and over again without re-creating them.

2. There is no geographic limit to selling your information. While most patients come to you within a certain radius, the Internet is instantly accessible to a global audience.

Your website not only acts as a place to present a solution to a problem, but it may act as a "storefront" where you can sell an information product to people that need your expertise. Consider the possibilities of marketing an ebook, supplement or non-prescription medical device from your website 24/7 without touching a product, fulfilling an order, answering the phone or filling out any insurance forms.

Your medical website has the potential to virtually print money. You promote your products by giving away valuable information as an introduction and then sell a comprehensive solution from your website. This can be delivered as a physical product in a box (DVD, CD and manual) or something that can be downloaded after purchase with a credit card or PayPal. If the information product is too large, then it can be delivered in a few weekly installments. People will pay you to save them time by organizing a vast amount of information into a "digestible" piece of information.

One of the most difficult things to adjust to when thinking about your medical expertise is the "reach" the Internet has. You are no longer limited to the typical geographical boundaries of a practice. If you can create something in text, audio or video format that has educational value or offers a solution to a problem, then you may have something to sell. You might have a training program for other physicians, or a supplement that you have compounded or a new angle on weight loss. I encourage you to "package" your expertise and sell it. You have worked very hard over the years to develop your body of knowledge, and it can really benefit people who don't have easy access to your practice.

One huge barrier to pulling this off effectively is underestimating your depth of knowledge in a certain area. You assume that everybody knows or has access to your information.

Nothing could be further from the truth. We all know the key to maintaining a healthy weight is proper nutrition and exercise, yet the weight loss industry rakes in billions of dollars annually with unique perspectives on the fundamentals.

I don't suggest selling anything disingenuous, of course. Your clarity and perspective is needed even more in this sea of noise. Provided you operate from a place of integrity, your products are needed more than ever *because* there is so much misinformation.

WHAT COULD YOU SELL?

Information products come in primarily three formats:

1. Text, like a manual, ebook or physical book

2. Video on a DVD or video downloaded or accessed from the Internet

3. Audio CDs that someone can listen to.

A book is a likely thing to sell. As the author of a book, your level of credibility will soar. You are officially a credible expert, and your "business card" is now a book! If you have written a book, that's great. If you want to write one, self-publishing has never been easier. And, with platforms like Kindle, you can even sell downloads of your book from your website. A traditional publisher is also a viable alternative. However, be aware: getting a deal with a traditional publisher is tough. If you are fortunate enough to get one, you will likely benefit from the publisher's editing and distribution channels.

If you don't want to write your own book, consider inter-viewing experts in a given field and be the "reporter" on a topic. These interviews may also be the makings of a DVD that might be worth marketing. It's very likely that you have access to someone worth interviewing. Your network and sphere of influence will be appreciated by your who might not be able to access and hear from someone in your network, without your sharing.

Manuals, books, DVDs and CDs can be sold separately or packaged together to strengthen the learning experience. There are commercially available companies that will package all of your products, as well as ship them, for a very reasonable cost.

Another way of selling something from your website is to create a subscription program. In this scenario, people join or subscribe for a set number of lessons. Or, just plan to create content on a monthly basis in exchange for a monthly subscription fee.

There are a couple of ideas here. If you have a complex topic or a topic that takes more time to implement (weight loss, cardiac rehab, etc.), it needs to be "chunked" into small, digestible pieces of information that can be interacted with over a period of time, say, twelve months. In this case, the subscription would have a definite start and end date. By creating lower monthly payments, you will pull in more subscribers and create a more sustainable income for yourself.

If you have a proprietary system, product or patent, you may have already considered a royalty-based income stream where subscribers pay a monthly fee to use your product.

People may need to use your product or ideas on a long-term basis (weight control), so they pay for a monthly subscription to get a monthly diet or exercise suggestion that includes a way for members to communicate and to support each other.

Ideas for the subscription/membership model are endless and can be a great boost to your income. Products of value vs. products that are empty promises are often easy to distinguish but difficult to describe.

By offering a high-quality product with case studies and other social proof, you set the bar at a high level and can realize an "annuity quality" income over time. Focus on value, not on hype.

Now, before you go off and create your first product, publish it on your website and buy your vacation home in Costa Rica, there are a few technical issues to address such as, "How do you collect payment online?" Enter the online shopping cart.

WHAT IS A SHOPPING CART?

If you have something for sale on a website, whether it be an information product (text, DVD, CD), or a subscription, there must be a place for people to pay for the item. The place they enter their billing and shipping information and submit payment is called a shopping cart.

A shopping cart is very important, because it must complete the financial transaction, while collecting other pertinent information such as address, state tax and shipping costs if there is a physical product.

People can pay with a credit card or PayPal using a shopping cart.

There are several shopping cart programs available, and almost all are paid for on a month-to-month basis. The shopping cart software is purchased by you and is integrated into your website by your web designer.

A shopping cart can also be custom-made by your web developer instead of using a premade, 3rd-party shopping cart.

AFFILIATES

If you want to begin with selling a low-cost product or one that you do not have to create yourself, there are others who have already created them and are eager for you to sell their product! In fact, many will pay you lucrative royalties for placing their product for sale on your website. You're not Wal-Mart yet, but you get the idea.

Online, we call these partners affiliates.

After your website is up and running, you can enlist affiliates to provide you with more products to sell. You can promote your own products through other affiliates.

So what is an affiliate? An affiliate is a person or company who will help you to market and sell your product in exchange for a percentage of the sale. In the information world, typical affiliate commissions are usually 50 percent.

Why would you want to give up 50 percent of your profit to someone else who has done nothing except do some promotion for something you created?

They may have their own list (you must have a list!) of people that is strategically aligned with what you have for sale. They don't have to create anything or do much work, and they can benefit financially by promoting your product to their list. What could be better for both parties? They get a percentage of something they didn't have to create, and you get exposed to a group of people you might otherwise not have access to.. Better yet, if people from the affiliate's list buy your product, they then become part of your list, without any advertising costs to you.

In 2012, I created an information product for people with lower back pain, called *Back Pain Relief – 7 Simple Steps*, which helps people rid themselves of nagging neck and back pain naturally. (Visit www.BackPainReliefInstitute.com.)

Originally created for chiropractors, this information product is in alignment (pun intended) with a supportive lifestyle advocated by many chiropractors. I thought that this $147 teaching course could act in harmony with their office treatment. I figured that a chiropractor might be interested in selling this product out of their office, so they could rest easier, knowing that their patients were getting a solid, three-hour education about what to do for themselves outside of the chiropractor's office. The benefit is that my course frees the chiropractor up to do things in the office for which they get paid, yet provides the education that the patient wants about a supportive lifestyle.

When the chiropractor sells this product, his or her patients receive a good education about lifestyle, and the chiropractor gets 50 percent of the $147 sale price.

The patient wins, the chiropractor wins, and I benefit as well. It is a triple win! The same idea goes for physical therapists treating spine pain. This product can also be licensed to larger organizations, like HMOs or Workers' Compensation. Entire industries have been created and grown from single ideas like this. Your product might not change the world, but it can transform enough lives to change your world. The opportunities are limitless.

Let's face it, people need to be taking a more active role in their healthcare, especially as costs rise to support "free" healthcare. Information products such as this one will help avoid costly encounters with the system. Rising healthcare costs will make it necessary for people to learn about their part in the disease process and take a more active role in the treatment of it.

Such a product shifts the cost to the patient, as well as empowers and challenges the patient to make appropriate lifestyle changes.

HOW DO I FIND AFFILIATES?

There is a shopping cart called Clickbank, which is connected to over 100,000 affiliates (individuals who are interested in promoting other people's products for a percentage of product selling price). There are dozens of other networks, but Clickbank is one of the easiest to get started with. They deal entirely with digital products (no supplements or physical goods).

Anyone with a list or an interest in lower back pain can participate in the sale of my back pain relief product. All an affiliate has to do is register, and then copy and paste one of my links (in this case, www.BackPainReliefInstitute.com) on their own webpage.

Clickbank does all the rest, including:

- Creating a unique code so my affiliate gets credit.

- Handling the credit card payment.

- Even handling refunds.

You may find an affiliate who can write great copy about your product and encourage sales on their blog. Recruiting affiliates helps everyone. I chose to use Clickbank to get easy access to their affiliates, to help promote my product and help me build my list at the same time. In the event that I create something else that might benefit this group, I'll be able to be in touch with them again.

In my case, the Clickbank shopping cart was integrated into my website by my web designer.

There are also pre-packaged applications that provide auto-mated solutions for the membership and subscription programs you may wish to offer.

ACTION STEPS

1. Recognize your knowledge and education and believe that you have something to share that is worth paying for. Under- stand that you may not be the first to publish this information on the Internet, but you could deliver it in a unique way. You could add more values and depth to your premium content, as compared to that available for free online.

2. Determine which format(s) you want to use to present your solution to the world's problem — ebooks, PDFs, videos, audios etc. It can be a one-time purchase or a monthly subscription.

3. Monthly subscription is ideal for medical products because, as we all know, treating or addressing a medical condition is a gradual process. It is often a series of steps to improve or cure.

4. Once you decide how you will share your knowledge, create your information product, package it (if it's a physical product) and then offer it on your website. Ask your web designer how to display it.

5. If you have something to sell, get a shopping cart for your website. There are several shopping cart providers, and they all function largely the same but have some different features.

6. Create an affiliate program or make your product available on affiliate marketplaces so that affiliate marketers can help you market and sell your products.

CHAPTER SIX

BENEFITS WITHOUT THE HEADACHES

Effectively leading a team alleviates the pressures of not just doing it all, but knowing it all.

What do you do when you want the benefits of a website without the headaches? Outsource it.

There are many available resources (such as Word Press) that allow you to create your own website, if you are so inclined. I only mention it because it's possible...but not recommended. I have had an Internet-based medical practice for over ten years and have never had the desire to create my own website.

Perhaps you have a friend, patient or relative who has offered to build a site for you.

Don't do it. Mixing business with personal relationships adds another layer that can impede your objectives. You can be friends with people in business, but pulling friends into your business can tarnish your friendship. You double the chances if they are related to you. Additionally, after your site is done, there are a host of ongoing tasks required.

- Are they going to maintain it?

- Who is going to update it?

- Can you ask for changes after it is completed?

- Who is going to link your social media to it?

- Can they update news and timely events on your site?

A website is never simply a "set-it-and-forget" situation. There is a certain amount of maintenance required with any of the changes that you make — and there will be changes, believe me. Someone with a comprehensive knowledge of website design is essential to all of your elements coordinating and working together well. Website creation is so much more than assembling some text, colors and a logo. If you do have an opportunity to peek behind the curtain, you will be surprised at the relative complexity and planning required when it comes to theme design, SEO integration, multiple pages and plug-ins, not to mention the addition of an autoresponder system, a blog, videos and a shopping cart... for starters.

Your time is better spent on deciding what content to incorporate into your website rather than how to incorporate it. One of the fascinating aspects about a website is that your site has the same opportunity to look as good as the Mayo Clinic website. The look and feel of a website is important to convey that feeling, sense of knowledge and trust that you want people to have in order to be comfortable with getting to know you online.

Ignore the pitches from anyone who says you can get a site up and online in minutes or even a few days. A medical website is not simply a static brochure. A properly executed site is a virtual extension of your reputation, knowledge and personality. It must be easy to navigate, with a consistent look and feel. Just as it is true with health, "curing" a sick website (one that is cheap and not designed for expansion) is much more costly than doing it right (prevention) in the first place.

I want to compliment you on completing this book. After reading it, you have started to learn about some truly important fundamentals:

- Medical marketing as an interactive education

- Driving traffic and engaging your audience

- Leveraging your website into a revenue stream

Knowing these fundamentals puts you at a different level of understanding and gives you new opportunities to build your medical practice: you know how to use your website to attract new patients and referrals, as well as to keep in touch with them. With the current technology available online, you can do more to educate patients than ever before, and you can now make your talents and expertise available to those who are looking for it, without geographical restraint.

You probably realize that, in addition to creating your content, you'll need to manage a designer, a developer and possibly a copywriter, through the several stages in order to produce a truly effective medical website.

Take it from me, as a medical doctor, your time and energy is too valuable to be spending in the trenches of website development. Your organizational skills will come in handy when coordinating your team of skilled professionals, though. Get help and be the captain of your ship.

I hope this book has shed some light on how your medical website can build and even transform your practice and enrich your life.

I invite you to visit www.MedicalWebsiteAcademy.com for additional resources and related products that may help you with your Internet marketing efforts.

— Tony Mork, MD

APPENDIX

THE MEDICAL WEBSITE ACADEMY

GLOSSARY

Affiliates – marketing partners that sell your products in exchange for a commission.

Algorithm – a set of steps that are followed in order to solve a mathematical problem or to complete a computer process.

Autoresponder – an email marketing service feature that lets you send emails automatically.

Blog – originally called a web log. A regularly updated website or section of your website that contains written posts (with the most recent post showing up at the top) on a particular topic or area of interest.

Header (website) – the upper part of a website that contains a banner, logo and the title of the website.

Information product – a product (video, audio or text file) that contains information or learning materials about a certain topic.

Keywords – a particular word or phrase that describes the contents of a web page. Keywords act as shortcuts that sum up an entire page. Keywords form part of a webpage's metadata and help search engines match a page to an appropriate search query.

Opt-in form – a form on a webpage that visitors fill out, usually with their name and email address, in order to receive updates, offers and free content. Opt-in forms are one of the most common ways to build a list.

Organic traffic – traffic that comes to a website via unpaid links from other websites, such as search engines like Google or Bing, directories, social media, blogs, etc. A website will tend to receive organic traffic as a natural result of its quality, as viewed by search engines and regular Internet users.

Paid traffic – traffic that comes to your website from online paid ad campaigns, such as Google AdWords.

Plug-in – a software module that adds a specific feature or service to a website. The idea is that the new component simply plugs in to the existing system. Plugins can extend WordPress to do almost anything you can imagine.

Pay per click (PPC) – an internet advertising method used to direct traffic to websites, in which you pay the publisher (typically a website owner or a search engine like Google) when your ad is clicked on their site. It is defined simply as "the amount spent to get an advertisement clicked."

Programmer – a person that creates computer software.

Reputation management – the process of identifying what others are saying or feeling about you or your business and taking steps to ensure that the general consensus is in line with your goals. Many people/organizations use various forms of social media to monitor their reputation, as well as monitoring ratings and reviews sites.

Search engine - a software system designed to search for information on the World Wide Web. Search results are generally presented in a list of results often referred to as search engine results pages (SERPs). The information may be a mix of web pages, images and other types of files. Search engines maintain real-time information by running a proprietary algorithm on a web crawler.

Search engine optimization (SEO) – strategies, techniques and tactics used to increase the number of visitors to a website by obtaining a high-ranking placement in search results.

Shopping cart – a piece of software integrated into a website that allows visitors to select items for eventual purchase and then to buy them.

Social media – websites and other online means of communication that are used by large groups of people to share information and to develop social and professional contacts.

Tag – a single word or group of words that best describes a blog post or article.

Tagline – 8-12 word phrase that explains the key benefits of your company. They can be set up as part of a logo or headline near the top of a website. Taglines are critical because people scan websites, especially first time visitors.

Template/theme – a pre-made skin or design that creates the outer appearance and basic functionality of a website.

Website – a group of linked pages on the Internet that contains information about a company, organization, person, government, products, etc.

Website designer - a person who plans, designs and implements basic website interfaces (layouts, colors, graphics, site organization).

Website developer – a programmer who specializes in creating websites and web applications. A Web developer is more focused on the way a website works than how it looks. His or her job focuses on the more technical aspects of a website, including the domain name, hosting, file uploads, building functionality and maintenance.

ABOUT TONY MORK

Dr. Tony Mork is a board-certified orthopedic surgeon specializing in endoscopic spine surgery, with a very successful 100-percent Internet-based practice. Dr. Mork is almost as passionate about the Internet as he is about helping his patients! With nearly thirteen years of experience using Internet marketing in his own practice, he is proud to bring you www.medicalwebsiteacademy.com.

REFERENCES

GENERAL WEBSITES & COMPANIES MENTIONED

Google AdWords – Google ads platform and keyword tool

Google Analytics – free service offered by Google that generates detailed statistics about a website's traffic

Keynote – Apple presentation software

Keyword Spy – keyword search and management service

WordPress – Content Management System (CMS)

PowerPoint – Microsoft Office presentation software

EMAIL MARKETING SERVICES

AWeber

MailChimp

iContact

GetResponse

Constant Contact

SOCIAL MEDIA/NETWORKING SITES

Facebook

Google Plus

Linkedin

Pinterest

Twitter

YouTube

WEBSITE THEME RESOURCES

DIY Themes

Studiopress

Theme Forrest

WordPress Theme Resources

Woo Themes

PLUGIN RESOURCES

Wordpress.org

RATINGS AND REVIEW SITES

Four Square

Google Plus

Health Grades

Insider Pages

Yelp.com

YellowPages.com

Vitals

SHOPPING CART SERVICES

1ShoppingCart

3DCart

BigCommerce

Paypal – not a full shopping cart but facilitates online payments

Shopify

Volusion

WEB HOSTING SERVICES

Bluehost

Fatcow

GoDaddy

Hostgator

Media Temple

SEARCH ENGINES

Bing

Google

Yahoo

AFFILIATE MARKETPLACES

Clickbank

Commission Junction

LinkShare

OUTSOURCING MARKETPLACES

Elance

Freelancer

oDesk

Made in the USA
San Bernardino, CA
16 June 2016